Extreme Producers:
Their Insights And Secrets

Extreme Producers: Their Insights And Secrets

Quick and easy-to-read ideas that will build your insurance and financial services career

Jerry Hraban

Premier Insurance Partners

Library of Congress Control Number: 2010912771
ISBN: Hardcover   978-1-4535-6705-0
                 Softcover   978-1-4535-6704-3
                 Ebook   978-1-4535-6706-7

Edited by Robert Fraass
www.RobertFraass.com

This book was printed in the United States of America.

To order additional copies of this book, contact:
Xlibris Corporation
1-888-795-4274
www.Xlibris.com
Orders@Xlibris.com
85924

Contents

"How am I going to live today in order to create the tomorrow I'm committed to?"—Tony Robbins

This book is dedicated to the many extreme producers across our great nation who have shared their insights and success secrets with me. Their wisdom is compiled in this book.

Foreword

In more than 20 years in insurance and financial services sales, I've had the privilege to talk with many of the top producers in the field throughout the United States. These producers, who routinely post huge sales numbers, have shared insightful sales and personal growth ideas that have enriched their personal and professional lives. I, in turn, have shared these success stories with many others, hoping they'll achieve greater success through this shared knowledge.

Several sales people have told me, "You should put all of those ideas in a book." That's how the seed for this book was planted. The book is designed to provide quick-and-easy moneymaking ideas that will help you achieve your dreams for yourself and your family.

Use the book in a way that works best for you—read it from beginning to end or flip through the pages to find the ideas that best work for you. Keep it close by so you can pick it up every day. I guarantee that you'll gain ideas and motivation to help you achieve your desires.

As you read this book, pay particular attention to the Action Steps. Answering the questions is important, because all of the top producers say that not only do they write down their goals, they write down concrete action steps to achieve them. Most people have long-term goals, but don't know how to reach them. This book will help you formulate your ideas and put on paper ways to advance toward these goals. You will better understand what you need to do today, this month, next month and next year to achieve your long-term dreams.

I encourage you read the book with a *pen*—not a *pencil*—and answer the questions as best you can. This book will help you generate ideas so you can develop your own ideas and Action Steps.

I wish you the best of luck in your career. If you come across success stories and sales tips you'd like to share with others, please visit my blog page at *www.pip1.com* and post them for others to read. I look forward to hearing from you.

—Jerry Hraban

Tip 1

Develop Mental Toughness

In every endeavor, in every line of work, in your professional and private life, mental toughness gives you the edge you need to succeed.

Everyone has something they are good at, but it's mental toughness more than talent that will give you an advantage. Mental toughness separates the good from the great. And it separates the great from the legendary.

Look at professional football and, especially, the position best known for requiring extraordinary mental toughness: the quarterback. Every QB in the National Football League has great ability; they wouldn't be paid to play football if they didn't. But what separates the good from the great is that ability to handle the demands of mastering a playbook and the mental demands imposed by the physicality of football, leadership of intricate teamwork and the confidence and knowledge to perform under pressure.

The classic example is the story of Ryan Leaf and Peyton Manning. Leading up to the 1998 NFL Draft, there was endless speculation about which fabulously talented quarterback would be selected first: Leaf or Manning. Manning or Leaf.

The Indianapolis Colts had the first pick in the draft and needed a quarterback. Which one would they choose?

To determine their selection, Colts' executives interviewed both quarterbacks, who both expressed how much they wanted to win and why they wanted to play for the Colts. The story goes that the defining moment came when they heard their candidates' vastly different answers to the same question: "If you are chosen by the Colts, what is the first thing you will do?"

Manning's reply was quick: "Study the playbook."

Leaf's answer? "I'm booking the next flight to Vegas so I can celebrate with my buddies."

Football fans know what happened to each young man. Manning became a Super Bowl champion and the league's most-valuable player. Leaf spent four disappointing years with the San Diego Chargers in a career plagued by poor performances, run-ins with teammates and the media and injuries. In short, he was considered one of the biggest busts in NFL history.

In the insurance business, 93 percent of those who become insurance agents don't stick it out past three years. These people who quit usually lack mental toughness. I've learned over the years that perseverance will win out—every time—over talent.

The insurance executives in the corner offices aren't always the most talented in the industry, but they are the ones who stuck it out when things didn't go their way. In the insurance and financial services field, a lot of people are just testing the waters. They want to see if this line of work can make them lots and lots of money.

The insurance and financial services professional who views this as a *career* usually has great success. That's because they happily work hard, coming to work early and staying late because they love what they do. Those who view this work as a *job* don't succeed. They work 8 to 5 and no more. That's because they *have* to work and not because they *want* to.

Career-oriented professionals eventually make a lot of money in our field. Those who view this as a job usually wash out. Which path do you want to follow?

Action Step: What steps will I take to persevere in my career when things don't go my way? Is my current occupation a "job" or a "career"?

_____

_____

_____

Tip 2

Pick A Product Specialty

As I've talked to top industry professionals over the past 20 years, I have found few who, in medical industry parlance, are "general practitioners." Just like doctors who develop a specialty, insurance and financial services professionals who make extreme amounts of money dedicate themselves to excellence in a narrow range of services.

The huge producers specialize: they only sell Medicare supplement insurance; they only sell annuities; they only sell life insurance.

But many think they should do more, more, more to make more money. "I do life insurance," they say, "so now I should sell car insurance." Or maybe they say, "I sell health insurance, so maybe I should branch out into annuities."

The big moneymakers don't do this *unless* a client comes to them with a special request. But that's not expanding product offerings. Rather, they are selling one specialty line and order-taking others.

So my advice is to become comfortable with that one specialty you sell best and learn it inside and out. Pick a specialty, too, based upon where you are at in your career. Some people say they would love to sell annuities, which are big-ticket items. But it's tough to ask a client to turn over, say, $60,000 to you when you are new to the business—and when your clients know it—and are struggling to just pay your rent.

Instead, it might be better to first work at selling easy-issue life insurance for which the average premium is just $60 a month. It's easy to ask for 60 bucks; it's a lot more difficult to ask for $60K.

Action Step: Which product do I understand best? Why does specializing in this product make the most sense for me?

_____

_____

_____

Tip 3

Need Help Specializing?
Study The Profiles Of Your Top Clients

Studying the demographics and lifestyles of your top clients is a great way to determine your product specialties. If you really boil down information about your top clients, you'll find that they have a lot in common: similar careers, similar age ranges, similar hobbies—maybe even living in a certain part of town.

Undoubtedly, you'll discover patterns in your clients' lives, giving you the opportunity to go out and prospect more clients like them. You might even learn that once you start studying your clients, you'll find you're an expert in a certain niche—a fact you didn't know before you did this important homework.

Action Step: What are the demographic and lifestyle commonalties shared by my top clients? How can I capitalize on these patterns?

_____

_____

_____

Tip 4

Find A Niche Market

Once you have selected an insurance or financial services specialty, next develop a clientele comprised of specific types of customers. Some insurance agents, for example, only sell life insurance, but then they go a step further and sell mostly to clients in just one occupation, such as schoolteachers or autoworkers. Others only sell annuities, but they only sell to senior citizens or Baby Boomers approaching retirement.

Focusing on one niche in the market (sometimes you'll hear it called an "affinity") gives you one distinct advantage—lots of referrals, which are *always* your best source of business in the insurance and financial services industry.

When I was young and fresh out of college, I really didn't know much yet about my industry. So it was hard for me to launch my career by offering bigger-ticket items, such as full financial planning services, mutual funds, etc. So instead, I selected teachers as my niche.

Teachers, in particular, often have products targeted just for them: tax-sheltered annuities, 403(b) retirement plans and other retirement-funding vehicles. These products allow you to go into a school with a ready-made plan to discuss. I found this strategy easy for me—easy to network and easy to get referrals.

Make a similar market niche strategy work for you to boost your networking power and referrals.

Action Step: Which niche in my market can I target with my products and services?

_____

_____

_____

Tip 5

Develop A Consistent Prospecting System

I talk with top insurance and financial services producers all the time. When I get the chance, I make it a point to ask them which techniques they use to achieve their success. Without question, here's the Number One answer: "I have a consistent prospecting system."

In other words, extreme producers have a reliable way to get their sales message in front of potential clients.

Some agents—never the top producers—reject the prospecting approach. "Well, I get a lot of referrals," they'll tell me. Now if you are getting a lot of referrals, that's great. It's the key to building a successful business. But I know very few agents who can live off referrals all of the time.

So, you need to develop a consistent way to develop leads. In the next three tips, we'll talk about three methods in particular: direct mail, customer-appreciation events and financial seminars. All are great tools for building your business.

Action Step: Which consistent ways to develop leads do I think will work best for me?

_____

_____

_____

Tip 6

Develop A Good Direct-Mail Lead System

If direct mail is such a great idea, why does it often not work? It's because most direct-mail campaigns are launched by low-end producers who drop just one mailing and then expect to see clients at their door, checkbooks in hand. That just does not happen.

Instead, do direct mailing like the pros who produce monster numbers. Those agents find a direct-mail lead carrier they like and let them bill their credit card on a recurring basis so they will drop mailings regularly, say every two weeks or every month. Then they commit to these mailings for at least six months. This gives your direct-mail campaign the time and repetitions needed to work.

One and done never works. Some top producers have multiple direct-mail campaigns running concurrently. I suggest talking to those producers about how they achieve success with this strategy.

When you are ready to sign on with a direct-mail firm, here's a strategy for getting the most bang for your buck:

Learn which day of the month your credit card company starts a new statement. That's the day you want to drop your mailing and to be billed by the sales leads company. That way, you have 30 days before you get your credit-card bill that includes your direct-mail campaign costs. Then, you have 30 days before you have to pay the bill. With this strategy, you have up to 60 days to pay for these leads.

Now, it usually takes about four weeks to receive your leads from the sales leads company. If you work these leads over the next four weeks, you can write some applications and earn commissions before the payment for your leads is even due.

If you do it right, you have a 60-day free loan from the credit card company. What a great way to pay for your sales leads without *any* out-of-pocket costs!

Action Step: Am I ready to commit to a three-month sales lead program and the success it can bring?

_____

_____

_____

Tip 7

Host Client-Appreciation Events
(And Make Sure Clients Bring Friends)

I am sometimes asked about client-appreciation events, such as dinners. Do they really work? You bet they do!

Here's a twist that can make such events even more effective. If you decide to invite your top clients to a golf outing, tell them that they must complete their own foursome to attend. Make the event special—hold it at a great course with plenty of amenities.

If your clients are avid golfers, they likely will show up. Now who do you suppose they'll bring to the event? Friends and family members who are just like themselves. By the end of the event, you'll chat with each client you invited and network with his or her three companions who are probably similar in age, social status and income. That's an easy way to build a great lead referral system!

If you invite 10 top clients who each bring along three people, you now have 30 potential clients—all of whom are referrals, which, once again, are always your best source of leads.

Not into golf? Do something similar with a dinner or tickets to a sporting event. Top producers use such client-appreciation events to get great referrals while giving clients a fun and memorable experience.

Action Step: Which type(s) of client-appreciation events would work best for me? Who are the clients I should invite who will bring me the best return on my investment?

_____

_____

_____

Tip 8

Hold Financial Or Insurance Seminars (If You Have The Expertise To Pull It Off)

Holding a financial or insurance seminar is a tried-and-true way to attract dozens of qualified prospects. Financial advisors have used seminars with great success for decades.

A financial seminar can take a lot of planning and coordination, but it can actually save you prospecting time in the end. Instead of discussing topics with clients and prospects one at a time, you have a captive audience that you can communicate with in a group setting.

Seminars position you as an expert in the field. If you provide good, objective information without an overbearing sales pitch, your clients and prospects will appreciate your knowledge. Plus, their trust in you will grow—a key part of building your personal brand, which we'll talk about later.

If you don't know where to start with planning a financial or insurance seminar, you'll find many reputable companies that offer consulting services for seminar marketing.

Seminars, however, aren't for the timid or inexperienced. You must believe in your message and possess good public speaking skills, which is certainly not everyone's strong suit. Plus, you must have genuine expert knowledge in the topics you are presenting. You will need to answer a wide array of questions from audience members, many of whom are on-guard against aggressive sales approaches and vague or incomplete advice.

When you are well prepared, seminars are a great way to get your message and name in front of many clients and prospects at one time.

Action Step: Are financial seminars a marketing tactic that's right for me? What are my areas of expertise that prospects and clients would take the time to hear?

Tip 9

Dig Up The 'Gold In Your Backyard'

Insurance and financial service professionals ask the same eternal questions: How do I get more prospects? What's the best lead system to use? Where do other top agents get their leads? I have learned that the Number One place to sell more business is right under your nose. Or, as I like to say, there's "gold in your backyard."

The "backyard" is simply your client files that you've built up over the years. If you are a product specialist (as I recommend) you don't necessarily know everything a client has in his or her portfolio. And you certainly don't know what they might be interested in buying. If you simply ask a client to buy more from you—or to buy a different product—you can generate a lot of income.

Say, for example, you specialize in annuities. Do you know if a client has certificates of deposit and their maturity dates? If you do, then you can talk to your clients at that time about how they next want to invest their money.

Ask your clients which company provides their life insurance. If they are interested in switching carriers, you can take that order, replace their insurance, and earn that commission. You also can see if they need more life insurance on their children. Or maybe they have grandparents to whom they will refer you. Just because you don't specialize in insurance doesn't mean you can't sell it to these clients. Your clients don't expect you to be an expert in everything. They will let you sell them products and even make good-faith mistakes along the way.

But what if you're not comfortable selling life insurance because it's not your specialty? Then bring in a trusted pro who does and split the commissions with that agent. That way, your client gets the needed coverage, and you get a commission plus a client who trusts you and who will turn to you when insurance and financial services needs arise. And don't forget, you are likely to get referrals from this client, as well.

Mining your client files for gold yields big results!

Action Step: What is my plan for reviewing my clients' files to help me sell more products?

_____

_____

_____

Tip 10

Hire An Assistant Or Intern

I talk to a lot of midrange producers who aren't high-end producers for one chief reason: they are on their own with no help whatsoever. Solve this problem by hiring a part-time assistant or intern.

To become a top producer, you need to allow people to help you. Many midrange producers hate to delegate. They aren't willing to loosen the reigns of control, and they aren't willing to pay. But if you, as a producer, are doing $8-an-hour work, you should instead hire a staffer who *wants* to do this type of work. Don't waste valuable time with busy work when you should instead be handling the heavy lifting—meeting people, working cases and bringing in the sales that fuel your business.

If you want to start small, that's just fine. Hire someone part time, say 10 to 20 hours a week, and work up from there. But you eventually need to turn over your paperwork, filing and customer service to a good staff. That's what the best producers do consistently.

Some midrange agents push back at this suggestion, telling me, "because I do everything, because a do a lot of handholding, *that's* why I have success." There might be some truth in that, but ask yourself these questions: Must *you* do the handholding, or can your *firm* handle that for you? You are Joe Agent Agency, but couldn't your assistant also represent Joe Agent Agency?

Turn your customer service over to your staffer. Then when a client needs help, ask the client, "Is it OK if I get back to you within the next 24 hours?" And, of course, it always is. Then the next time your part-time staffer is in the office, have him or her complete the follow-up work.

Your clients still get great customer service, and your time—your company's most-valuable asset—is freed up to perform the prospecting and selling that drives your company's success.

Action Step: What are the goals I hope to achieve if I decide to hire a part-time staffer or intern? Which tasks do I want a staffer or intern to perform?

_____

_____

_____

Tip 11

'Duplicate' Yourself

Many top-producing agents and financial services pros have learned the value of "duplicating" themselves.

Duplicating takes two forms:

1) Hiring an assistant to perform tasks that you don't have time to do or don't want to do (described in Tip 10).
2) Hiring sales people to work for you.

On your own, you can only make so much money—there are only so many hours in a day. But duplicating yourself will help you move your organization forward. If you can find good people to duplicate your tasks, then they make money, and you make *more* money.

Let's say the staffer you hire can turn out only 50 percent of your production. But that still means, at the end of the day, that you are 150 percent ahead. People you hire won't do everything exactly the way you do or want it to be done, but hire those who you think will accomplish what you need. Who knows, someday they might become better than you!

I have found that midrange producers often struggle to take their business to the next level because they don't duplicate themselves—they don't want to give up that control. They can't allow themselves to buy leads from someone else, or they can't picture others working with their clients.

Say, for example, you specialize in annuities, but want to add more life insurance to your mix of business. But perhaps you just don't have the time or needed expertise. After all, there's no need to break the principals I discussed in Tip 2.

In that case, hire somebody who can handle your life insurance business and pay them according to their experience and how much revenue they produce. Then pay them *more* as they become *more* valuable to your business.

Duplication is how *all* organizations grow!

Action Step: Which steps should I take to duplicate myself so my business will grow?

_____

_____

_____

Tip 12

Start Your Own Agency

After years in the profession, you might start to see yourself as a coach to other insurance or financial services professionals beyond just working as a personal producer. If so, think about creating your own agency as a way to powerfully grow your business.

This is the ultimate way to "duplicate" yourself many times over. Plus, you'll find satisfaction in leaving a legacy—your business can provide people an income and their life's work long after you are gone. As an individual sales producer, your business will die when you do. But if you start an agency or corporation, your work can live on forever.

Starting your own agency might seem daunting, but the process is actually easier than you might think. But where do you start?

I invite you to visit the Premier Insurance Partners website at *www. PIP1.com* to learn more about how to launch your own agency. Then feel free to contact me so we can discuss your ideas about starting an agency and how I can help.

If you want to help people in your profession grow as you grow right along with them—if you see yourself as a coach rather than a player on a team—I encourage you to explore the possibility of starting your own agency.

Action Step: Do I see myself as more of a player or a coach in my profession? (If you see yourself as a coach, research how you can start your own agency, including contacting me at Premier Insurance Partners.)

_____

_____

_____

Tip 13

Embrace Technology

Many find learning and implementing technology in their businesses hard. It takes time, effort and money. Plus, you are an insurance or financial service professional—you didn't get into this career to learn computer software or design websites. Many times, that type of activity just doesn't interest people in our profession.

Although learning technology can seem like a time- and money-waster in the beginning, it's a time- and money-saver in the end. You don't have to read tons of dry technical manuals. Instead, check out websites, such as *Lynda.com*, to learn the latest software by watching videos that teach software skills rather than reading user manuals. Google "learn software online" to find other such websites.

And, again, if you don't want to learn technology yourself, hire part-time help. College interns are a great way to go. They cost little and are highly literate in computer technologies. For that small amount, you can make your business technically advanced, saving time and money and providing better service to your customers.

Action Step: Which computing technologies do I need to learn to improve the success of my business?

_____

_____

_____

Tip 14

Build Your Personal Brand

If you've worked in the insurance or financial services business for any length of time, you've discovered one fact: it's a jungle out there!

Your marketplace is crowded with hundreds of financial pros scrambling after many of the same clients and the same dollars. So how do you stand out from the crowd?

The big buzzword in business today is "personal branding," and for good reason. With the advent of online social media, it's the best way for clients to learn about you and your services so they know they can entrust their business to you. If you don't think about how to best promote yourself, your values, personal mission and unique attributes to clients and prospects, you'll be at a disadvantage when marketing your brand to others and attracting the right clients.

Once you've identified your strengths and interests, the next step is to put the pieces in place to enhance your brand in your community. Here are the best ways to accomplish this:

- Create a great website that clients and prospects can find easily.
- Take advantage of social media websites such as Facebook, Twitter, LinkedIn and YouTube. Video is an increasingly popular and powerful communication tool.
- Hold client-appreciation events and financial seminars so people get to know and trust you.
- Get involved in community causes and efforts. They help paint a positive picture of you and your office as you give back to the community.

There are nearly endless online resources and great books about personal branding. A couple of the best books are "Me 2.0: Build a Powerful Brand to Achieve Career Success," by Dan Schawbel, and "Career Distinction: Stand Out by Building Your Brand," by William Arruda and Kirsten Dixson. You can order both books online from national booksellers.

Writing this book is part of my personal branding effort to help people learn about my expertise in the financial services industry. Figure out what you do best and which unique attributes you can offer prospects and clients to develop your own personal brand.

Action Step: Which social media websites make the most sense for my business? What unique qualities and values do I have that I want to communicate to my prospects and clients?

_____

_____

_____

Tip 15

Hire A Social Media Manager

One of the best things I have done for my business is to hire a social media manager. She works for me in another city for 20 dollars an hour at up to 20 hours a month. That might sound like a lot of money, but because she's a contractor (no paid benefits)—and because I only pay her as needed—it's a surprisingly reasonable cost to help build your personal brand.

Your social media manager can live anywhere. I have never even met mine in person.

If you don't understand how social media can help your business, you need to learn. These websites are effective and inexpensive tools for building your personal brand and the brand name of your business—keys to successfully earning the respect and trust of your clients.

But establishing and maintaining a social-media presence, and doing it right, can be time consuming. That's why, like hiring a part-time staffer, employing a freelance social media manager is a better use of your time than handling it yourself. A social media manager will get your name and business before the right people on LinkedIn, Facebook, Twitter, YouTube, etc.

You need to become familiar enough with social media to give your social media manager direction. There are hundreds of resources on the Web to help you get up to speed. You don't want the social media expert you hire to go off in a direction you never intended because you didn't give him or her enough guidance. Still, be open to their new ideas that you might not have considered.

Social media is an important tool for reaching potential clients through its powerful networking capabilities. Use this new technology to its fullest to help build your business.

Action Step: What do I want to accomplish with my social media strategy? If I hire a social media manager, how can he or she add value to my business and personal branding efforts?

_____

_____

_____

Tip 16

Manage Your Day The Night Before

In my experience, I have found that the best insurance and financial services producers run their businesses better in many ways than small-time producers. One key difference I continually see is that top producers have a plan for each day—and that they devise these plans the night before. That's when they decide what they will do and how much time to devote to each task, making their days more efficient and profitable while reducing stress and wasted energy.

Poor producers don't have a plan. They come into each day helter-skelter, reacting to events rather than proactively setting the tone for what they want and need to get accomplished.

Be like a top producer: create a to-do list the night before. That way, it's on your mind when you go to bed. I even find you can think about your list and what you need to do while you are sleeping. If you wait until you arrive at the office to make your list, it's too late. Your day starts to take advantage of you before you can tackle what you have planned.

It's all about being proactive rather than reactive. Reactive tasks, which are a part of conducting business, are for your internal staff. Reactive people get paid a small salary. Proactive people get paid the big money. That's why you want to proactively run your business and have your staff handle the vital reactive stuff that keeps your business humming.

Action Step: In addition to creating to-do lists, what else will I do consistently to plan for each workday?

Tip 17

Plan Your Day Using Time Blocking

Select the right tasks for the right time of day and the right time of the week. This means scheduling tasks for times that work best for you as well as your clients. Ask yourself when, for example, you will be scheduling appointments. Then pick the block of time every day or the days of the week that will work best.

The next step is to ask yourself when you will plan to make prospecting calls and perform related prospecting work. Select the times of the day or week when you know your prospects are most likely to be available to conduct business.

An important task to schedule is your busywork—the needed paperwork that keeps your company running but that doesn't make you any money. Be sure this type of work isn't scheduled in "prime time," the key business hours that should be devoted to making money. Busywork should be performed during slow times with customers, such as on Friday afternoons and early in the morning, like between 7-9 a.m., before you see clients.

Action Step: Which tools will I use (day planner, calendar, scheduling software, etc.) to ensure that I am performing the right tasks at the right time of day?

_____

_____

_____

Tip 18

Don't Mistake Activity For Achievement

The memorable motivational thought "don't mistake activity for achievement" comes from John Wooden, the legendary college basketball coach who died at age 99 in 2010. I have a friend who likes to say something similar: "Don't mistake activity for productivity."

Either way, the important message is the same: Being busy doesn't mean you're doing the right things at the right time. You need to have your to-do list as I've discussed and focus on the work you need to perform to achieve your goals, eliminating tasks that don't help you achieve success.

Action Step: What will I do to motivate myself to focus on activities that help me achieve success?

_____

_____

_____

Tip 19

Build On Your Strengths By Hiring Someone To Cover Your Weaknesses

How many times have you heard, "You need to improve your weaknesses"? How many times does a child bring home a report card filled with A's and B's only to be criticized by his or her parents for that one C?

It's totally inaccurate to think that progress will come from improving what we are not good at. What happens when you work on your weaknesses? You don't improve a lot, and it's no fun.

If you're not a good swimmer, and I tell you to hit the pool every day because it's your weakness, you'll learn to hate swimming, and you'll dread practice. You might improve your stroke a little, but you'll never be a great swimmer. But, on the other hand, if you are a fabulous long-distance runner, and I teach you how to become a marathoner, then you're going to love practicing, and you'll quickly become a better runner.

Likewise, in the insurance and financial services industry, if you hate follow-up and customer service, hire staff to perform those tasks. You will find there are people who *love* to do this type of work that you dread. They love helping customers, completing reports, or filing and other administrative work.

Odds are, you don't like administrative work, or you wouldn't be reading this book. When a task is not your strength, even though you know it's vital work, you will keep putting it off and putting it off and it won't get done in a timely manner. And when it finally *does* get done, it won't be completed correctly.

Look at large companies: some people do marketing, others are in sales, and still others are accountants, administrative staff and so on. These people like what they do and, therefore, do it well. But you'll never take a salesperson and turn him or her into a successful administrative assistant. And since you yourself would not take a job as an administrative assistant, then hire someone to perform that task for your business. Everyone will be happier and more productive.

The best tools I've seen for discovering your strengths—and the strengths of those who work for you and with you—are the "Strengths Finder" books and website from the Gallup Organization. The book and website (*www.StrengthsFinder.com*) are used together to assess your strengths and what you can do best. Gallup's strengths assessment program is widely popular among Fortune 500 companies and other organizations of all types. I encourage you to take the Strengths Finder test as a way to learn about your best skills and how to put them to work for you.

Action Step: What are my strengths and how can I enhance them? If I am unsure of my strengths, I will use Strengths Finder materials or another self-help guide to discover them.

_____

_____

_____

Tip 20

Record Or Write Down Your Thoughts

The phenomenon has happened to all of us—maybe it's when you're driving down the road or when you wake up in the middle of the night. Regardless of when it happens, great ideas and light-bulb moments that pop into your head often are gone just as quickly unless you have a way to permanently record them.

That's why you should keep a tape recorder or even just a notepad in your nightstand, in your car, or wherever you usually are when inspiration strikes. It's an effective way to keep track of your great ideas.

I learned this early in my career. I now record my thoughts on the built-in recorder on my cell phone. With the advent of smart phones, you have a recorder in front of you at all times. Or, sometimes I will call my cell phone and leave a message on my voice mail—any way to create a permanent record of my inspired thoughts.

Cell phone, tape recorder, notepad, or just the back of a napkin—whatever works for you, devise a way to track your good ideas when they pop into your head.

Action Step: How will I record my great ideas so I don't forget them?

_____

_____

_____

Tip 21

Keep Work Fun

A top producer once told me many years ago that everyone has ups and downs, even within the same day. When work got stressful or difficult, he would pull a joke book from his desk to get a few laughs. He said it put him in a good mood and helped him keep the stresses of life in perspective. And as he talked with his staff or customers during the day, he would share a joke and a laugh, lightening their mood as well.

Read a joke of the day, have a joke or humor book handy or visit a website that makes you laugh and gives you a short break from work. When you are frustrated and want to slam down the telephone, you'll find that laughter is the best medicine.

In life, it's important to keep things light. It's good for your outlook; it's good for your heart and soul; and it's good for your business.

Action Step: Which books or other resources will I use to take a break during the day to lighten the mood at work?

_____

_____

_____

Tip 22

Keep Work Fun For Others, Too

As I always tell the people in my company, I want working at Premier Insurance Partners to be fun. I recognize that my coworkers would rather be with their kids—or, as the bumper stickers say, they'd rather be fishing or golfing—than working with me all day.

But if you must go to work, let's make sure this place is enjoyable. I don't want my employees dreading coming to work every day. If they do, I hope they'll find another job that they love instead.

Action Step: What are activities and morale-boosters I can plan for my employees to help keep my workplace fun?

_____

_____

_____

Tip 23

And If Work Isn't Fun, Find Something That Is

You'll make much more money if you enjoy your career; that's a statement proven by research. If you find yourself in a job where you dread going to work every day (and if that feeling lasts more than a few weeks) it's time to find a new position.

I've been there and done that. I once had a job making great money, living a good life by most standards. But when I got out of bed every day, the stress had already started to well up in my gut. That's because as time wore on, I found I didn't like the job anymore, and it certainly wasn't fun. I knew I had to make a change.

Remember, though, that not liking a job is not the same as failing to do what's required to succeed. Every job has tasks that are not enjoyable but that must be done. Don't switch jobs or careers because you think you can avoid unpleasant tasks. Every job has them.

Action Step: Do I dread going to work every day? If so, what can I do to either improve my job or find a new calling that will make work fun and rewarding?

_____

_____

_____

Tip 24

Focus On Work At Work And Family At Home

One of the best things I've learned over the years is focus—and not just focus during work. Whatever you are doing, no matter what it is, devote your energy to it instead of splitting your attention among the different issues and responsibilities in your life.

In other words, work time should be for work; family time should be for family; vacation time should be for vacation. Don't let work intrude when you are with your family or taking a much-deserved break.

In the past, I would go on vacation and never relax—I thought I should be making calls or prospecting. But now when I am with my kids, my attention is on them, not my job. I don't check my e-mail, and I don't play with my smart phone; I give them the attention they want and need.

And when I am at work, I try to minimize distractions. I make it a priority to not goof around, surf the Internet for fun or procrastinate. When I am at work, I am working.

Action Step: What can I do to improve my focus—both at home and at work?

_____

_____

_____

Tip 25

Write Down And Refer To Your Goals

The best insurance and financial services producers, without question, all have goals. And not only do they set goals, they write them down.

Personally, I record goals that I want to accomplish in my life, and I look at these long-term objectives frequently. When I do this, I'm surprised how many goals I wrote down 20 or so years ago that I have actually achieved—often in a timeframe I didn't think possible.

I have learned that if you write down a goal and refer to it frequently, it will be on your mind all of the time. That will spur you to start talking to people about your goals, and then—sometimes slowly and sometimes quickly—they become reality. People you run into at work or at parties or wherever will help you meet your goals, maybe in small ways or maybe in large ways.

Here's one of the first goals I wrote down when I launched my career: Start a company in which I can help people become successful and make good money. Premier Insurance Partners has become just that—a great company with employees and marketers earning a good income.

My goal became a reality, but I had to work toward that goal for 16 years until I started Premier Insurance Partners. Everything I did leading up to launching my business involved working toward this goal.

But you will never obtain your goal if you don't write it down and look at it all of the time, turning your goal into a burning desire in your head. As someone once told me, if you look at the goal over and over, the words will burn themselves on the inside of your eyelids. Every time you blink, you will see them.

Your goal will be front and center. The goal you see all of the time is what you will work toward.

Always set goals and write them down—no matter how crazy they might seem.

Action Step: What are my long-term goals? I will write down my goals and refer to them frequently so they are always on my mind and so I can react when opportunities arise.

Tip 26

Update Your Goals

Think hard about what you really want to achieve. Once you reach some goals, what then? Or, perhaps, circumstances change, and what was once a goal no longer makes as much sense. Don't stick to meeting goals if they are no longer relevant. Change them to what you truly want.

Nothing is better than crossing off goals on a list. That's why I love to-do lists, because you check off items as you achieve them. Just think how rewarding it would be to set big goals and then make it a point to reflect on them as you mark them off your list.

Never erase your goals; just put a line through the ones you have met. This will surely serve as motivation to meet your goals, both big and small, and to set even more ambitious ones heading forward.

Action Step: Which goals do I have that are no longer relevant? If I have outdated goals, I need to think about how they can evolve and write down my new, adjusted goals.

_____

_____

_____

Tip 27

Be Persistent

For 15 years, a poster has hung in my office featuring this quote: "The difference between a successful person and others is not a lack of strength, not a lack of knowledge, but a lack of will."

NFL legend Coach Vince Lombardi, a name that's synonymous with success, spoke those words.

There is one thing I know more than all others: to succeed, you must be persistent, and you must have a strong will. I'll go out on a limb and say there is someone smarter about computer systems and software than Bill Gates. But that person wasn't persistent enough to overcome the obstacles Bill Gates did to build a Microsoft Corporation.

There are certainly people who are smarter than you are, but you have achieved more. And I am sure you know people in high places who you think are total idiots, but they have had more success than you have. Maybe they had just enough smarts, and, most of all, maybe they were very persistent. Maybe they wrote down goals and kept moving toward them. What they lacked in pure intelligence, they made up for in other intangible ways that fueled their success.

It's never the smartest person who becomes president. It's someone who sets their goals and smartly works their plan during their political campaigns. Running for political office is a great example of a situation where the smartest person doesn't always win. The winners are those who can best handle adversity.

Become a businessperson whose persistence and tenacity translates into success.

Action Step: What motivation do I need to always be persistent and strong as I pursue my goals?

_____

_____

_____

Tip 28

Believe In Yourself

A friend once told me, "My favorite quote is, 'I have to believe in myself when no one else does.'"

This advice is vital. You must have supreme confidence that your actions and plans will take you where you want to go. Develop a strong faith in your business, your business model and your business plan.

Like most Nebraskans, I love the excellence and tradition of the University of Nebraska football team. Bo Pelini, the Cornhuskers' head coach, likes this motto: "Believe in the process." He emphasizes that if you develop a sound process that everyone buys into, you will achieve success. Games will be lost, but long-term success is assured when everyone confidently moves in the same forward direction.

When you have a vision of what you seek to achieve, always, always, always keep the faith. Too often, people give up on their dreams when success is right around the corner. They become afraid they can't make it when the situation instead calls for fearless determination. Believe in yourself, and success will be yours!

Action Step: How will I motivate myself so that I don't give up on my goals when success might be just around the corner?

_____

_____

_____

Tip 29

Finish Strong

In addition to "believe in the process," another core principal of Coach Pelini's philosophy is "finish strong."

In football, this means working hard in practice and not letting up in the last 15 minutes because you are tired and know it will be over soon. Players need to continue to get stronger as the practice comes to a close.

In business, it means working until the end of the workday. I continually tell my coworkers to finish strong. It's 4 o'clock, I'll say. Don't waste that final hour because quitting time is near . . . finish strong!

A friend shared a story about visiting a company to call on a business acquaintance. During the conversation, the colleague peered out of his office and said, "Well, it must be 3 o'clock."

My friend replied, "How do you know it's 3 o'clock?"

"I can look into the hallway and see that people are really starting to move," the man replied. "We call this the 'cubicle tours.' Because at 3 o'clock, the lower producers in the cubicles get up and start socializing, because they know that if it's 3 o'clock, then 5 o'clock is just around the corner. These are the producers who won't be here for long."

Don't get caught participating in cubicle tours. You are wasting valuable time that can help you get ahead in your business. Just like a football team, never give up until the clock winds down to zero.

Action Step: Which habits can I develop that will ensure I finish strong each day?

_____

_____

_____

Tip 30

Start Strong, Too, By Making Your 'Easy' Calls

The most difficult part of any endeavor is getting started. "It's the *start* that *stops* most people," one of our top marketers is fond of saying.

Think about your daily routine. The hardest part might be getting out of bed in the morning when you're feeling tired. And when you get to work, diving into your tasks can be difficult because there are people who want to socialize and e-mail messages you may be tempted to wade through before you can dig into the day's essential tasks.

The key to success in sales is talking to clients and prospects. And if you spend too much time with e-mail, procrastinating and socializing, your ability to obtain success in your career will be limited.

To get started, schedule your time based upon the to-do list you created from the night before (see Tip 16)—and stick with it.

Here's a good technique I've learned: Start the day by making some "easy" calls. We all have clients you need to talk to who know you, like you and are good customers who you know will call you back if they are available. Make some of these calls first thing in the morning to get your day off to a good start.

But at the same time, hold back some of your easy calls for times when you hit a rough patch. In sales, there are always times when events don't go your way. When that happens, return to your list of good customers and make those calls. They will put you back in a good mood. Sprinkling easy calls amongst your more difficult tasks is a great way to stay motivated and upbeat about your job.

Action Step: How can I change my routine so I get started *immediately* each day?

Tip 31

Be A Puppy

"Be a puppy" is one of my favorite ideas to share with people. I got this from a producer who once told me, "Whenever you meet someone, you need to be like a puppy."

So what does acting like a puppy entail?

When someone comes home, the puppy jumps up and down, excited to see its owner—maybe even running around the room.

Now you probably shouldn't run around the room or jump into people's laps when you meet them, but you need to be excited to see everybody. That's because if you are excited, they will be eager to see you as well. And if you *aren't* excited to see someone, that person will react the same way—they won't be thrilled to meet with you.

Get excited when someone walks into a room; it makes a difference. It sets the tone for any occasion, whether it's a lunch or business meeting or if you're meeting your future spouse. An upbeat greeting sets the tone for what follows.

When you come home, be excited to see your kids and spouse. Are they more thrilled to see their puppy, or are they more excited to see you? If the dog wins out, it's time to change your attitude.

Action Step: Do I set a positive tone with people in the workplace and at home? If I need to improve, what should I be doing differently?

_____

_____

_____

Tip 32

Praise Customers Often

Praise the people around you. I can't say this enough!

Send clients thank-you notes and greeting cards to express your gratitude for their trust in you and your business. At my company, we *always* thank our customers for their patronage.

"We truly appreciate your business," we say. "Now how can we help you today?"

Remember that you earn the most money from repeat customers. And praising customers and providing great customer service are the best ways to keep them coming back.

Action Step: How can I better show my customers that I appreciate their business?

_____

_____

_____

Tip 33

Put Your Face On Your Business Card

When you put your photo on your business card—and when people keep the card where they can see it, such as on their refrigerator—they will see your face every day.

And this is a proven statement: If your clients see your photo often, they will think they've seen you face-to-face more frequently than they actually have. Clients will feel like they know you better, even if you've never met them or have had just one or two appointments.

So put your face on your business card, your brochure, your website and all of your marketing materials. You'll find that when you call, your clients will perceive that they know you well and feel more comfortable around you. And that, of course, can lead to more sales.

Action Step: How can I get my name and my photo on more marketing materials delivered to more prospects and clients?

_____

_____

_____

Tip 34

Buy From Yourself

I recently read about a business owner who decided to buy products from his own company, just to see how his experience would be. The result? His eyes were opened. Buying from his company wasn't pleasant at all. He found the process cumbersome.

Always own what you sell. If you're in the insurance and financial services industry, you'll find that you will sell *much* more when you completely believe in your products. Make some purchases and pay close attention to the process. Is it easy to buy from your company? If not, then fix it.

Another story I've heard involved a company that sold products online. When the owner and his employees bought their own stuff over the Internet, they found the process difficult. There were just too many steps.

Now if the owner found buying online hard, how could he convince his customers that the process was efficient and easy? Buying from himself helped this business owner improve his company.

Action Step: How do I feel about my company's customer service when I buy my own products? What improvements could enhance the customers' experience?

Tip 35

Ask For The Order

When closing a sale, remember that it's "ask and ye shall receive." In other words, always ask to take a client's order. I've found that most low-end producers don't close sales well. They don't know how to ask, and, often, they don't even remotely try.

If you can say, "Can we write this up today?" that's great. And if you have a better way to say it, such as, "Is there any reason why you wouldn't buy this from me today?" then do that. Do your sample closes; do your trial closes. But no matter what, make sure you ask for the order during every appointment.

Here's the question I like to pose to producers: "Are you asking for the order, or are you a professional conversationalist?" Many in the insurance and financial services industry meet a lot of people, but, too often, that doesn't translate to money in their bank accounts. These people are simply professional conversationalists—they are not helping themselves, and they certainly are not helping potential clients.

Don't be shy about asking for the sale. Be a salesperson, not a professional talker.

Action Step: What steps can I take to become better at closing sales?

_____

_____

_____

Tip 36

Do Those Things That Failures Refuse To Do

A mentor once shared with me this maxim: "Successful people do those things that failures refuse to do."

Over the years, I have found this simple quote explains much about why some people succeed and others fail.

One habit that successful people adopt that others don't is waking up early and putting in long hours when needed. If you try to run a business by only working 8 to 5, you won't make your fortune. Failures are good at completing easy tasks, but refuse to do or procrastinate about difficult ones they dislike. It's not like successful people love unpleasant chores, but they know they must be accomplished before they can obtain their vision for their company or career.

You see this all of the time in athletics. Athletes at the top of their game are usually the ones who go beyond what's asked of them by their coaches. They run extra wind sprints and lift weights when it's not required. They are driven to perfect their fundamentals, pour over playbooks and study film of opponents.

Likewise, if you go the extra mile that others won't, you'll achieve success and pass by those lacking the gritty determination needed to match your accomplishments.

Action Step: Am I doing the unpleasant tasks I need to succeed? If not, what's holding me back from working harder and smarter as I strive for success?

_____

_____

_____

Tip 37

Ask People For More

When making a sales call, emulate the upsell techniques used by fast-food restaurants. What are you always asked when you place an order? "Would you like fries with that?" Or, "Would you like a soda with that?" Or maybe, "Would you like to make this a Value Combo?"

These restaurants succeed by always looking for just a little more business, especially in these cases where they have a captive audience at the counter or drive-through window. And just like fast-food joints, if you always ask your customers for a *little* more, you eventually will get a *lot* more!

Asking for that additional sale opens the door to satisfying your clients' other unmet insurance and financial services needs. Not everybody, of course, will take you up on your offer. In fact, many will say no. But plenty of clients will say yes, too. That's why you need to ask every client with whom you are working for that little bit extra.

Don't be afraid to ask. It's a key to your successful practice.

Action Step: How can I improve my upselling techniques so that asking for a little more will add up to a lot more?

_____

_____

_____

Tip 38

The 'Columbo Close'

Do you remember the '70s and '80s TV detective show "Columbo"? That popular drama's trademark moment came when the police investigator, Lieutenant Columbo as portrayed by Peter Falk, would use his disarmingly polite charm to gather information from a potential witness or crime suspect.

As he wrapped up an interview with civil thank-yous, Columbo would reach for the doorknob before turning around and saying, "Oh, there's just one more thing . . . ." This last question would help him gather even more information. This is the same tactic as asking, "Would you like fries with that?"

When your meeting draws to a close, stop your client and ask, "Oh, there's just one more thing. By the way, are you satisfied with the interest rate of your bank's CDs?" Or maybe the question is "Who has your cancer insurance?" or "Have you upgraded to this new type of life insurance?"

This last-minute question isn't about the product you came to sell, but it gets your clients thinking about their need for the product and opens the door to selling them more during your next appointment.

Action Step: Which questions can I ask clients and prospects that would work as a "Columbo Close"?

_____

_____

_____

Tip 39

Becoming A Millionaire Isn't Rocket Science, But If It Was Easy, Everybody Would Be One

Making money isn't necessarily easy, but making a lot of money isn't necessarily rocket science. Savvy entrepreneurs can become millionaires selling insurance, working in real estate, operating a sandwich shop—these and many other occupations you probably never thought would earn people that kind of money.

None of those occupations are overly difficult to pull off. But those who are successful work very hard and, as we've discussed, work hard at accomplishing the tasks they need to succeed—the tasks that failures refuse to do.

Everyone gets discouraged, and sales professionals understand there will be peaks and valleys. But successful people in financial services, insurance and many other occupations know that if they focus on their vision, they will achieve their goals and the financial rewards that come with them.

Action Step: Am I working hard enough to ensure that I meet my goals? If not, what should I do differently?

_____

_____

_____

Tip 40

Hire A Business Or Life Coach

Hiring a "coach" to help you achieve your career and personal goals is a great investment in yourself and will improve your chances for long-term success. A good life or business coach can help you overcome procrastination and other stumbling blocks that prevent you from becoming all you can be.

One coach I really like is Sarano Kelley, who wrote "The Game: Win Your Life in 90 Days." I found that his process for providing the tools and structure for creating success can produce amazing results. I encourage you to read the book, which you can order online from national booksellers, and learn more about Kelley and his work at *www.saranokelleycoaching.com.*

Another business coach I can't say enough about is Maribeth Kuzmeski, the founder of Red Zone Marketing (*RedZoneMarketing.com*). She is a former public relations expert for a pro basketball franchise who now teaches other organizations and individuals, primarily in the financial services industry, how to market themselves just like a professional sports team. She has been a tremendous asset for my career, and I highly recommend her materials to anyone wanting to achieve success in financial services or insurance.

Action Step: Do I need a business or life coach? What do I want a coach to help me improve?

_____

_____

_____

Tip 41

Read Motivational Materials

I am a firm believer that you need to read motivational materials frequently. Why wouldn't you take the opportunity to pick the minds of the world's best motivational speakers and thinkers?

Often, people say they don't have time to read at length. But if you read 45 minutes a day, you can get through books fairly quickly. When you are truly short on time, there's plenty of free motivational material online. Print a few pages and take a few minutes to study the content. You'll find that good motivational thinking will put you in the proper mindset for success, an invaluable trait in both your professional and personal life.

Many sales organizations start out the day or week with a motivational meeting. I recommend you do the same to "fire up the troops" and keep yourself sharp and inspired.

And, of course, you need read this book and keep it handy. My whole purpose for writing and sharing these ideas is to share my passion for getting the most out of life and to help you understand what successful people do to achieve their vision. And one thing successful professionals do, I've discovered, is to regularly read motivational materials.

Need a place to start? I recommend "Awaken the Giant Within" by Anthony Robbins, a fantastic guide to achieving what you want in life. I was visiting the office of a successful producer, and I noticed this title on his bookshelf. The title jumped out at me. Robbins has his books for sale and plenty of motivational material on his website: *TonyRobbins.com*.

Action Step: Where can I find the motivational books and other materials that will work best for me? Write down the titles you want to read.

_____

_____

_____

Tip 42

Do Something You Think Is 'Impossible'

If you, like me, are approaching those midlife crisis years, you might start making your "bucket list"—a list of those accomplishments you want to achieve before you "kick the bucket." If you decide to make such a list, include one item that, right now, you consider "impossible." Setting this goal and working to achieve it will invigorate, motivate and excite you as you take your life to a new level of understanding and accomplishment.

A great example of someone achieving the "impossible" is a friend whose family members are all strong swimmers. My friend, however, was the exception. She feared swimming for years, but as she approached age 50, she decided it was time to overcome her trepidation and learn how to swim with her family.

Now, most middle-age people fear putting on a swimsuit, much less learning how to swim. But through her determination and by hiring a good swim instructor, my friend can now swim with her kids and husband, who are so proud of her and her accomplishment.

So what impossible thing do you want to accomplish? Maybe instead of swimming, you dream of completing a marathon, learning a new language or musical instrument—maybe writing a book.

Many people these days seem attracted to competing in a triathalon to prove their mettle. A great place to start is the *BeginnerTriathlete.com* website. It's a great resource to take you through everything step-by-step that you need to learn and how to train. There's even a "Couch Potato to 5K" program designed to get non-athletes off the sofa and striving to complete a 5-kilometer (3.1-mile) race.

No matter what you choose for your "impossible" goal, know that you'll be able to find the resources and inspiration to reach your achievement.

Action Step: When I set aside my preconceive notions about what is and isn't possible, which "impossible" accomplishment would I most want to achieve? Which steps will I take to make this a reality?

_____

_____

_____

Tip 43

Do As You Would Advise Others To Do

Most everyone has a good sense of what others should do in a given situation. The funny thing about people, though, is that many don't apply that same logic to their own circumstances. If we all would take the advice that we readily offer others, we'd all be highly successful. I firmly believe we have an innate ability to make decisions that lead us down the right path. We simply must act on our own advice.

Most people know what they should do, but fear and uncertainly keeps them from acting on their internal dialogue. Do yourself a favor—take your own advice and conduct your life as you would advise others to do.

Action Step: What advice do I give others that would make my own life better if I followed it?

_____

_____

_____

Tip 44

Take Responsibility For Your Life And Success

If you've read the previous 43 tips, I think you'll see that a theme has developed: Everything that you must do to achieve success requires action, discipline, follow through and, most of all, responsibility.

A top producer from Utah once told me, "If you ever think life has dealt you a tough hand, read about the life of Mahatma Gandhi." A more recent example is the story of NFL player Michael Oher in "The Blind Side" memoir and 2009 hit movie.

In your professional life, no one will hand success to you; you must go out and earn it. Sure, outside influences you can't control can play a role in your success or failure—that's just a fact of life. But a large majority of what happens to you—good or bad—can be traced to your decisions and actions.

Responsibility means owning your achievements and failures, and you are sure to have some of both. But whatever you do, don't blame others when you fall short. Some people blame others when things go wrong, pinning their failures on others' actions.

Often, you'll hear people blaming their parents for raising them wrong or abusing them. Life doesn't deal everyone a fair hand, but you can overcome obstacles primarily by taking responsibility for your life and your success. Once you genuinely accept responsibility, you'll often find that your situation improves immediately.

One of my favorite sayings is, "If it's meant to be, it's up to me."

Truly believing this statement and accepting that this is how life operates will surely change your attitude and the success you achieve in both your career and personal life.

Action Step: What feelings do I have about how others have contributed to my failures? How do I overcome this negative mindset to accept responsibility for my own success?

_____

_____

_____

Tip 45

Be Comfortable Being Uncomfortable

Early in my career, one of my mentors taught me the following: "If you are comfortable, you are stagnant. If you are uncomfortable, you are growing."

Tony Robbins once conveyed the same idea when he was asked in an interview, "If you could give the people listening to this discussion one piece of advice, what would it be?"

Tony's answer: "Go do something today that scares you. Go do something that makes you uncomfortable."

Not surprisingly, doing the uncomfortable quickly becomes comfortable. Then you try something new, and the cycle starts over.

Trying the ideas in this book that are new to you will surely make you uncomfortable. Maybe, for example, you decide to try "The Colombo Close" (Tip 38). This sales tactic will definitely be uncomfortable the first time or two, but eventually it will become second nature at all of your appointments.

Action Step: Which idea in this book will I start with immediately?

_____

_____

_____

Tip 46

Act!

I end with one of the most important traits of wildly successful professionals: They act! They pull the trigger!

They don't wait and outthink themselves. They decide and move forward even though they know corrections must be made along the way. Just like any journey, there will be roadblocks and setbacks, but starting *today* is what's needed to achieve success.

Now that you've worked your way through this book, the next step is to take action. Do it today!

Action Step: What will I do *today* to start my journey toward success?

_____

_____

_____

Let me know how I can help you!

Now that you have read "Extreme Producers: Their Insights and Secrets," let me help you realize your potential in the field of financial services and insurance. Contact me soon about one or more of our following services:

☐ Our next National Sales Training Camp
☐ Maximizing your efforts in the senior insurance market

    ☐ Annuities
    ☐ Medicare supplement insurance
    ☐ Medicare Advantage
    ☐ Life insurance

☐ Learning to prospect like the pros
☐ Speaking at your training event
☐ Selling more through seminars
☐ Maximizing your sales through direct mail
☐ Writing and editing services (publish your own book or newsletter; copywriting for your website)
☐ Learning how to start your own insurance agency
☐ Other: _____

_____

_____

Name _____
Address _____
Phone _____
Best time to call _____
E-mail _____
E-mail this information to me at *jhraban@pip1.com.*

Or, fax or mail this form to:

Premier Insurance Partners, LLC
1015 N. 204th Ave.
Omaha, NE 68022
Fax: 402/408-1498
Phone: 800/504-7471
www.pip1.com

Made in the USA
Middletown, DE
10 January 2019